First World War
and Army of Occupation
War Diary
France, Belgium and Germany

32 DIVISION
14 Infantry Brigade
King's (Liverpool Regiment)
51st Graduated Battalion
14 March 1919 - 31 October 1919

WO95/2394/2

The Naval & Military Press Ltd
www.nmarchive.com
Published in association with The National Archives

Published by

The Naval & Military Press Ltd

Unit 10 Ridgewood Industrial Park,

Uckfield, East Sussex,

TN22 5QE England

Tel: +44 (0) 1825 749494

www.naval-military-press.com

www.nmarchive.com

This diary has been reprinted in facsimile from the original. Any imperfections are inevitably reproduced and the quality may fall short of modern type and cartographic standards.

© Crown Copyright
Images reproduced by permission of The National Archives, London, England, 2015.

Contents

Document type	Place/Title	Date From	Date To
Heading	WO95/2394 Mar-Oct '19 51 Kings Liverpool		
Heading	Lancashire Division (Late 32nd Divn) 14th Infy Bde (1st Lancs Infy Bde) 51st Bn (King's) L'Pool Regt. Mar-Oct 1919		
War Diary	Dunkerque	14/03/1919	16/03/1919
War Diary	Beuel	17/03/1919	31/03/1919
Heading	War Diary April 1919		
War Diary	Beuel	01/04/1919	30/04/1919
Miscellaneous	Action of Troops in Case Riots in Beuel	02/04/1919	02/04/1919
Miscellaneous	51st Battalion The King's (Liverpool) Regiment.	13/04/1919	13/04/1919
Miscellaneous	Location Of Guards.		
Miscellaneous	Orders For Reserve Force-Move To Assembly Position.	26/04/1919	26/04/1919
Miscellaneous	Copy No 12	26/04/1919	26/04/1919
Miscellaneous	Orders For Reserve Force-To Move Forward.	26/04/1919	26/04/1919
Miscellaneous			
Miscellaneous	Reference Order for Reserve Force move to Assembly Position.	30/04/1919	30/04/1919
Miscellaneous	Reference Order for Reserve Force move to Forward	30/04/1919	30/04/1919
Heading	War Diary May 1919		
War Diary	Beuel	01/05/1919	31/05/1919
Miscellaneous	Orders For Reserve Force Move To Assembly Position.		
Miscellaneous	Orders For Reserve Force To Move Forward.	19/05/1919	19/05/1919
Miscellaneous	O.O. "A" Company.	31/05/1919	31/05/1919
Operation(al) Order(s)	51st. Bn. The Kings (Liverpool Regiment.) Order No. 1.	28/05/1919	28/05/1919
Heading	War Diary June 1919		
War Diary	Beuel	01/06/1919	18/06/1919
War Diary	Boisdorf	19/06/1919	20/06/1919
War Diary	Stossdorf	21/06/1919	30/06/1919
War Diary	Beuel	30/06/1919	30/06/1919
Operation(al) Order(s)	51st Bn The King's (Liverpool Regiment) Order No. 2 Appendix A	17/06/1919	17/06/1919
Operation(al) Order(s)	51st Bn The King's Liverpool Regiment Order No. 3 Appendix B	19/06/1919	19/06/1919
Operation(al) Order(s)	51st Bn The King's (Liverpool) Regt Order No. 3 Appendix C	29/06/1919	29/06/1919
Miscellaneous	Message Form.		
Heading	War Diary July 1919.		
War Diary	Beuel	01/07/1919	31/07/1919
Heading	51st Battalion The Kings (Liverpool) Regiment War Diary August 1919		
War Diary	Beuel	01/08/1919	03/08/1919
War Diary	Stossdorf	04/08/1919	31/08/1919
War Diary		22/08/1919	26/08/1919
Operation(al) Order(s)	51st. King's Liverpool Regiment Order No. 5 Appendix A	31/07/1919	31/07/1919
Operation(al) Order(s)	51st. Bn. The King's Liverpool Regiment. Order No. 6	05/08/1919	05/08/1919
Operation(al) Order(s)	51st. Bn. The King's (Liverpool) Regiment. Order No. 7	29/08/1919	29/08/1919
Heading	War Diary 51st. Bn. The King's (Liverpool) Regt. Period 1-30 Sept 1919		

War Diary	Stossdorf	01/09/1919	05/09/1919
War Diary	Bonn	06/09/1919	30/09/1919
Operation(al) Order(s)	51st Bn. The King's Liverpool Regiment. Operation Order No. 8	31/08/1919	31/08/1919
Miscellaneous	Guards Found By 51st. Bn. The King's Liverpool Regiment.	19/09/1919	19/09/1919
Miscellaneous	1st. King's Brigade.	27/09/1919	27/09/1919
Heading	War Diary 51st. Bn. The King's (Liverpool) Regt. Period October 1919		
Miscellaneous	51st. Bn. The King's Liverpool Regiment Operation Order. By Lieut. Colonel J.O. Widdows, M.B. Bonn. 16/10/19	16/10/1919	16/10/1919
War Diary	Bonn	01/10/1919	16/10/1919
War Diary	Obercassel	17/10/1919	31/10/1919

WO 95/2394
Mar - Oct '19
SI Kings Liverpool

LANCASHIRE DIVISION
(LATE 32ND DIVN)
14TH INFY BDE (1ST LANCS INFY BDE)

51ST BN (KING'S) L'POOL REGT.

MAR - OCT 1919

WAR DIARY 51st King's or Liverpool Regt.
INTELLIGENCE SUMMARY

(Erase heading not required.)

Army Form C. 2118.

Vol I

Place	Date	Hour	Summary of Events and Information	Remarks and references to Appendices
DUNKERQUE	14/3/19	4 p.m	Disembarked from England	
	15/3/19	1 p.m	Departed for Germany (Route: BERQUES, - AMEKE - CASSEL, - MERRIS, - BAILLEUL, - STEINWECKE, - ARMENTIERES, - LILLÉ. Crossed BELGIUM during night of	
	15/16/3/19		proceeding valley of MEUSE, - NAMUR, - LIÈGE, crossing German frontier during night of	
	16/17/3/19		near AIX-LA-CHAPELLE, - COLOGNE), arriving at	
BEVEL	17/3/19	6.30 am	Then billeted in BEVEL + outskirts.	
BEVEL	18/3/19		Captain F.R.C.H. BUCHANAN, R.A.M.C. reported to replace Captain A.S. HEBBLETHWAITE, M.C. R.A.M.C.	
"	20/3/19		Captain A.S. HEBBLETHWAITE, M.C. R.A.M.C. departed for England for demobilization	
"	28/3/19		2/LIEUT. H.B. PARRY, 7th King's Liverpool Regt. reported.	
			LIEUT. H.B. SPENCER, 1/6th " " " reported.	
			LIEUT. S. LEE, 17th " " " reported.	
			A/CAPTAIN J.H.M. LITTLE, M.C. 1/6th King's Liverpool Regt. reported.	
"	29/3/19		2/LIEUT. L.H. NICHOLSON, 1st King's Liverpool Regt. reported.	
"	30/3/19		LIEUT. K.O.B. POCKLINGTON, 1/6th " " " reported.	
BEVEL.	31/3/19.			

H.J. Lewinsday
Major
for
O.C. 51st King's Liverpool Regt.

# WAR DIARY or INTELLIGENCE SUMMARY

Army Form C. 2118.

War Diary
April 1919

OC O'Smith
Lieut Colonel
51. Kings Liverpool Regt

WAR DIARY
INTELLIGENCE SUMMARY
(Erase heading not required.)

Army Form C. 2118.

Instructions regarding War Diaries and Intelligence Summaries are contained in F. S. Regs., Part II. and the Staff Manual respectively. Title Pages will be prepared in manuscript.

51st King's Liverpool Regt.

Place	Date	Hour	Summary of Events and Information	Remarks and references to Appendices
BEUEL	1/4/19		The following Officers reported a/Captain J.S. ADDY M.C. & a/Captain H. DRAKEFORD M.C. 7th King's Liverpool Regt.	
	2/4/19	9.30 a.m. to 6 p.m.	Half Battalion steam trip up the Rhine. BEUEL to COBLENZ.	
	3/4/19		Captain E.H.G. ROBERTS, M.C. reported. 9th King's Liverpool Regt.	
	4/4/19		Lieuts. H.S. WILSON & J. WORSLEY, M.C. departed for England for demobilization.	
	9/4/19		Captains W.P. HART & J.R. ELLIS departed for England for demobilization.	
	10/4/19		2/Lieut. J.E. HICKS departed for England to be demobilized.	
	11/4/19	23.40	1 Platoon standing to until resume normal at 11.10 12th instant.	
	12/4/19		CHAPLAIN REV. M.J. DUNN (R.C.) reported. 2/Lieut. J.S. ANDERSON 1st King's reported.	
	12/4/19		Attached orders issued in case of riots.	"A"
	13/4/19		" " " for flying patrols &c.	"B"
	15/4/19	9.30 a.m. to 6 p.m.	Half Battalion river trip up Rhine BEUEL to COBLENZ.	
	16/4/19		Lieut. Col. O.O. BORRETT, C.M.G., D.S.O. reported & assumed command of Battalion.	
	18/4/19		The following Regular officers departed for England: Captain A.G. NEWMAN, Cheshire Regt. 7 Lieuts. H.S. HOSEASON, C.N. CLARKE, P.R. O'SULLIVAN, & R.M. MORROW, all Liverpool Regt.	
	21/4/19		Lieut Colonel W. ADAM, D.S.O. left for demobilization.	
	23/4/19		The following Officers reported from the 53rd King's Liverpool Regt.: Lieuts: R.J. VENN, J.H. L. OWEN, H. BUSH, F.H. KING, 2/Lieuts. J. ROBERTS, & C.E. BILLINGTON.	

WAR DIARY or INTELLIGENCE SUMMARY

Army Form C. 2118.

Instructions regarding War Diaries and Intelligence Summaries are contained in F. S. Regs., Part II. and the Staff Manual respectively. Title Pages will be prepared in manuscript.

(Erase heading not required.)

51st King's Liverpool Regt.

Place	Date	Hour	Summary of Events and Information	Remarks and references to Appendices
BEUEL	26/4/19		Attached orders issued in event of move to Assembly Position and move forward	"C" "D"
BEUEL	27/4/19		Major H.G. Lewis Day proceeded to Cologne to sit on board enquiring into War Materials. Capt Gifford attached proceeded to Cologne for duty on Summary Court.	KD
BEUEL	28/4/19		Inspection by Divisional Commander at Hangelar. Battalion returned to Camp at 18.30 hours. Captain W.C. Moran & Capt H.G. Rathbone reported from Hospital.	KD
BEUEL	29/4/19		30 OR proceeded to RAOC Cologne 6 OR Brigade Signal Course. 91 Divisional Orch. 3 Riding horses proceeded to Collecting Station Cologne.	KD
BEUEL	30/4/19		OC Brigade School & Light Trench Mortar Battery took up positions for the defence of Beuel in the case of Riots. The Commanding Officer inspected the positions & with certain alterations found all correct & gave instructions for this practice to take place each month.	
		1500	Instructions issued at 1500 hours for a practice to take place in case the Battalion received instructions to move to Assembly Position at 0800 hours on 1 May. Amended instructions to Move to ASSEMBLY POSITION.	E KD F & G

'A'

Action on Threat in case of Riots in BONN.

1. Riots may occur:
   (a) In BONN and its district alone.
   (b) In BONN zone.
   (c) In both BONN and BAD GODESBERG simultaneously.
   (d) In either (a) (b) (c) in conjunction with action on or inside the perimeter of the Divisional defence lines.

2. In answer the above cases the scheme for the defence of BONN bridge should be in Appendix II of the Divisional Defence Scheme comes into force at once. As regards (b) the action taken is laid down in appendix III of Divisional Defence Scheme.

3. The main points of civil and military importance in and near BONN which it is necessary to protect are:-
   (i) The railway bridge over the main road leading out of BONN. The destruction of this bridge could not be effected quickly or without explosives, but it would not only prevent the use of the railway but completely block one of the only two means of access for traffic between BONN and BAD GODESBERG.
   (ii) The bridge over the railway between BONN and BEUEL. The destruction of this would have a similar effect to that of the bridge at (1).
   (iii) The main railway station at BONN. In this area is included the Depot of the Electric Railway in KESSENICH, BONN. Only tramcars are stored there and all electric power is obtained from BONN. The Depot of the electric railway is not in itself therefore a point of essential importance though its destruction might cause much inconvenience. The blocking of the main lines and the destruction of the railway station and goods there would be more serious.
   (iv) Rathaus. KAISERPLATZ, BONN. This contains the office of Civil administration and must be protected. Six reliable German police armed with revolvers are maintained here.
   (v) The gasworks, Maarflacken, outside BONN town on the road to JESSENICH. Five reliable Germans (unarmed) are maintained here who if armed would assist in the defence.
   (vi) Waterworks Pumping Station at ALTENAHR near KOENIGSWINTER. The destruction of this would take out of most of the water supply of BONN but it would take time and is unlikely as an immediate objective of an attack.

4. Other places of importance which are however either not vital or unlikely to be attacked at once, are:-
   (i) Schaafhausen'scher Bank, FRIEDRICHSTRASSE, BONN. This would not be easily attacked and would be defended by three reliable German police armed with revolvers.
   (ii) Community Cash Bank, WILHELMSTRASSE, BONN. Not easily attacked. Defended by three reliable Germans armed with revolvers.
   (iii) Waterworks basin at ALTENAHR (hill) above KUDINGHOVEN. Unlikely for early attack and difficult to damage quickly and seriously.
   (iv) Subway under railway bridge, WILHELMSTRASSE, BONN. Its destruction would interrupt main railway, but approaches can be watched from the bridge in para 3 (i). Destruction would require large quantities of explosives and take a considerable time.
   (v) Branch Office of the District Savings Bank, 22 BAHNOFSTRASSE, BONN.
   (vi) Local Sick Insurance Society, 10 KAUNPLATZSTRASSE, BONN.

- 2 -

(8) Bahnstrasse Railway Station, REICHSTRASSE, BUHL.
(9) Track of main Railway from/to ROKASUL through BUHL to ALSDEN.
(9) Track of BRONITARBAHN Railway from BUHL to HANGTLAR.
(10) Savings and loan cash Society. KAISER.GEWERXEVEREIN.
31. ORTGRUPPE; KUDINGHOVEN.
(11) Savings and Loan Cash Society. KAISER CONRADSTRASSE VILICH RHEINDORF.
(12) Savings and Loan Cash Society. OBERDORFSTRASSE.

Of these (1) - (2) might be early objectives of rioters but a small mobile force should be able to give sufficient assistance to the defending German police if action is taken quickly.
To (5) and (6) the same applies, but they are of minor importance. If hostile attack is threatened at any of the remainder, such action should be taken at once by the O.C. the nearest Troops as may appear desirable, but Troops should not be sent except for a definite object and in sufficient force.

5. In the event of a riot commencing or being threatened, information will at once be sent by any officer to:-
 (a) Battalion Headquarters.
 (b) Town Commandant BUHL.

On the receipt of the message the alarm will be sounded by all Guards in BUHL.

6. On the alarm sounding or a riot being imminent, all individual soldiers will return at once to their Units. Should "Lick" return he is impracticable owing to rioting or blocking of Roads, they will report at once to the nearest of the Division for orders.

7. On the alarm being sounded, "B" Company will at once move and protect the in ortant points named in para 3. O.C. "D" Company will reconnoitre these and forward a copy of suggested dispositions to Battalion Headquarters by 6.p.m. on the 15th inst. Most of these points can be best observed and kept under fire by day by the occupation of the high ground at the quarries, just south of the Gas Works.

Signallers must attend with this Company.

O. i/c of Signallers will make arrangements for establishing a Station for receiving and transmitting any message.

A picquet must be maintained covering the main Road and Railway from OBERCASSEL, near the Gas Works.

One platoon must be kept in mobile reserve by O.C. "D" Company.
All Officers will reconnoitre all places mentioned in paras 3 and 4.
"A" "C" and "D" Companies will stand to in or near their billets 8. (i.e piston billets or alarm posts) Each Company will send two orderlies to report to the Town Commandants Office.

In case of riots Company reserve ammunition will not be issued, and all Officers must realise the importance of obtaining "uick possession of the points mentioned and getting the upper hand before the rioters plans mature.

10. Battalion Headquarters details will assemble at the Pioneers Shed.

11. Reports will be sent to the Town Commandants Office, BUHL.

-:o:0:o:-

(Sgd) H. J. RATHBONE, Capt & Adjt.
51st Bn The King's (L'pool Regt)

Copies to:-
1. O.C. "A" Company.   7. I.O.
2. O.C. "B" Company.   8. T.O.
3. O.C. "C" Company.   9. Signals.
4. O.C. "D" Company.   10. Bill.
5. O.C. H/Q Headquarters. 11. M.O.
6. S.O.   12. for Diary.

SECRET.

51ST BATTALION THE KING'S (LIVERPOOL) REGIMENT.

COPY NO.

Reference 1st. King's Brigade No. G.1/1/19.

---

1. (a) 1 Officer, 3 N.C.O's. and 9 O.R. will be detailed for duty from Inlying Picquet each night for Patrolling Battalion Area.
   (b) The Officer will sleep at 27 BONNERSTRASSE, and N.C.O's. and men in the Regimental Guard Room.
   (c) O.C's. Coys. will arrange for blankets to be sent to Guard Room.
   (d) A flying patrol of 1 N.C.O. and 3 men will visit each Company Guard, Battalion H.Q. Guard, and H.Q. Guard of 13th King's every two hours, commencing at 2000 hours.
   (e) On return they will report All Correct or otherwise.
   (f) In event of any disturbance the commander of the nearest Company Guard will be warned, the commander of which will be responsible for warning his O.C. Coy. who must investigate and forward a report to Battalion H.Q.

2. Company Guards must be warned of these patrols, and informed as to what times they are expected.

3. Dress for Patrols:- Drill Order.

4. Patrols dismount at Reveille.

5. In the event of a Riot the remainder of Inlying Picquet would report to Officer in charge at the address given above.

6. Any civilians found out of doors after 9. p.m. must produce a pass. Failing this or a pass suspected to be not of order, the person must be conducted to Guard Room and detained, report being made to O. I/C Patrol.

7. Officers must carry revolvers after dusk when away from their billets.

8. Attached list giving location of Guards.

---

1. O.C. "A" Coy.
2. " "C" "
3. " "D" "
4. " "M" "
5. Commanding Officer.
6. Transport Officer.
7. File.
8. War Diary.
9. 13th. King's.
10. R.S.M.

BEUEL. 13.4.19.

[signature] Capt.

LOCATION OF GUARDS.

"A" Company.	Nil.
"C" "	153 VLICHSTRASSE and 2 KIRCHSTRASSE.
"D" "	86 BOHNERSTRASSE.
"E" "	Guard Room 24 VLICHSTRASSE. Boat farm yard.

ORDERS FOR RESERVE FORCE - MOVE TO ASSEMBLY POSITION.

1. On receipt of the order "positions" the Reserve Force will concentrate at the Assembly Position in and about NIEDER HOLTORF with Force H.Q. at the School of cross roads in S.D. corner of square 17.

2. The Force will consist of:-
   1. 51st. Bn. The King's (Liverpool Regt) from BEUEL.
   2. 2 Batteries R.F.A. (8 guns) from RAMERSDORF.
   3. Platoons X Corps Cyclists from BONN.
   4. Section R.E. from BONN.
   5. Section Machine Gun Battalion from
   R.A.M.C. from.
   O.C. Reserve Force.   O.C. 51st. Bn. King's.

3. It is calculated that the Force should be concentrated at the Assembly Position within 4 hours of receipt of "Position".

4. The following measures will be taken by 51st. Bn. King's on receipt of orders to prepare to move:-
   (a) Packs, blankets, and other spare kit will be stacked at the theatre in BOLKERSTRASSE (now) occupied by "D" Coy, and placed under a Guard of 1 N.C.O. and 6 men.
   (b) All surplus Officers and O.R's. will assemble at the Orderly Room under the Orderly Officer. The Senior Officer will take command, and report to O.C. Brigade School and assist in the defence of BEUEL.
   (c) All Company Transport will report at Coy. H.Q.
   (d) Ammunition to complete 120 rounds per man will be issued.
   (e) The Battalion will parade in "Fighting Order" with unexpired portion of the days rations in the mess tin.
   (f) Cookers will carry one days rations.
   (g) Companies will report to Orderly Room when ready to move. Other units will conform as far as it concerns them.

5. On the order being given to move the Battalion will march to NIEDER HOLTORF. Starting point. 200 yards E of first house in PIDZOHEN on the BEUEL-PIDZOHEN road.
   Order of March. H.Qrs., "A", "B", "C", "D", Companies. Remainder of Transport in rear of Battalion. Lewis Gun limbers and cookers will march in rear of their respective Companies.
   Report Centre. Head of the Battalion.
   Cookers. According to time of day cookers will be making tea or a hot meal during the March.

6. Advance Brigade Headquarters will be at the School House, ROLEBER.

Acknowledge.

23.4.19.

Co. ndng 1st. B. Liverpool Regiment.

O C Smith
Lt Colonel
IT Commandg Regiment

Distribution:-

1. 1st. K'gn. Brigade.
2. Commanding Officer.
3. 2nd i/c Coy. Cmd.
4. Adjutant.
5. }
6. } All Companies.
7. }
8. }
9. Transport Officer.
10. Quartermaster.
11. Intelligence Officer.
12. R.F.A.
13. R.F.A. 138 Brigade
14. 90th. Field Ambulance.
15. R.E. 203 Field Coy.
16. X Corps Cyclists.
17. Machine Gun "D" Coy.
18. File
19. War Diary
20. War Diary.

SECRET.

Copy No. 12

In the event of the Battalion receiving the Order "Positions" not more than 34 officers will proceed:-

Headquarters -
    Commanding Officer.
    2nd. in Command.
    Adjutant.
    Signalling Officer.
    Intelligence Officer.
    Medical Officer.
    Transport Officer.
    Orderly Officer (Mounted).

Companies.
    6 per Coy. with the exception of "A" & "C" who will take 7.

26/4/19.

O.C. Smith
Lt.Colonel,
Commanding 51st. Bn. "The King's" (Liverpool) Regt.

DISTRIBUTION.

Copy No. 1. Commanding Officer.
2. 2nd. in Command.
3. Adjutant.
4. Signalling Officer
5. Intelligence Officer.
6. Medical Officer.
7. Transport Officer.
8.)
9.)
10.) All Coys.
11.)
12. File.
13. War Diary.

ORDERS FOR RESERVE FORCE - TO MOVE FORWARD.

1. On receipt of orders to move forward the Reserve Force will move forward and occupy the ridge at UCKERATH.

2. The advance will be made by a series of bounds, the first bound being to WESTERHAUSEN and the high ground near SAND and WASCHPOEL.

3. The Force will move off in the following order:-
   - Cyclists.
   - "A" Coy.
   - "B" "
   - 2. Batteries. R.F.A.
   - "C" Coy.
   - "D" "
   - R.E.
   - Machine Gun Section.
   - R.E.
   - R.A.M.C.

4. The Cyclists will move with all speed and occupy the ground mentioned in para 2.

5. "A" & "B" Coys. will move on and occupy WEBBERHAUSEN via STIELDORF, HECCKERCTH, DURMROTH, FEDCNWINKEL, BLANKENBACH, OSTERHAUSEN.

   "C" & "D" Coys. will move on and occupy the high ground at SAND & WASCHPOEL via STIELDORF, STIELDORFERHOHN, HEISINGHOUSEN, OBERFLIES, SAND.
   The Artillery will be prepared to cover the advance from position near DURFROTH.
   The Machine Gun Section will support "C" & "D" Coys. and will also be responsible for the right flank of the force.
   R.E. & R.A.M.C. will move via STIELDORF/HOHN to OBERPLIES when the above mentioned position is occupied.
   Signals. A Station will be established at ROTH. Report Centre will move via STIELDORFHOHN, HEISINGHOUSEN and OBERPLIES.

6. When this bound has been completed a halt will be made and the batteries will move forward to cover the next bound.
   Officers will reconnoitre with a view to a further move forward which will be made by the two supporting Companies leap-frogging and will be to the vicinity of the line HUCHEL-BRUICH.
   The Cyclists will move forward as soon as the Infantry are established in the WESTERHAUSEN-SAND line to reconnoitre the crossings of the River HAN.
   Report Centre will move to high ground above WELMSBERG.
   R.E. & R.A.M.C. will move from OBERPLEIS along the WELMSBERG road.

7. The next bound will be to the final objective viz; the UCKERATH ridge and the high ground at PRIESTERSBERG. Unless required in support the leap-frogging Companies, the Companies at HUCHEL and BRUICH will hold that line as a support line to the final objective.
   Artillery positions will probably be South of WELMSBERG.
   O.C. Machine Gun Section will dispose his guns to cover the outpost Report Centre near HOVE.
   R.E. & R.A.M.C. WELMSBERG.

8. When the final objective has been reached the O.C. Cyclists will detail one section to establish communication with the left Brigade along the STIMEL-SUCHTERSCHEID road, and two sections to establish communication with the American Division at GRIESENBACH-LINDSCHEID line and contact patrols towards the American Division and the left Brigade.

   The leading Companies will push forward officer patrols towards the GRIESENBACH-

P.T.O.

9. Acknowledge.

S.L.E.
23.2.19.

Co..anding 1st. B. Liverpool Regiment.

[signature] O.C.Smith
Lt.Colonel.

Distribution.

1. 1st. King's Brigade.
2. Commanding Officer.
3. 2nd i/c Command.
4. Adjutant.
5. }
6. } All Companies.
7. }
8. }
9. Transport Officer.
10. Quartermaster.
11. Intelligence Officer.
12. R.F.A.
13. R.F.A. 158 Brigade.
14. 90th. Field Ambulance.
15. R.E. 203 Field Coy.
16. X Corps Cyclists.
17. Machine Gun "D" Coy.
18. File.
19. War Diary.
20. War Diary.

OPERATION:- On Thursday 1st May a pratice of the action to be taken on receipt of the code word Advance.

The practice will commence at 0800 without further orders from his office.

Kits and Transport must not be packed before 0800.

The Battalion will move to their assembly positions at NTR HOLTORF, but not beyond it.

TIME II.— Breakfast:- 0700.
Dinners to be cooked on way and eaten at NIEDER HOLTORF.
Reminder of days rations carried on the man.
Arrangements to be made for H.Q. meal to be cooked on "A" Coys. cooker.

In accordance with orders for Reserve Force move to Assembly Position.

Coys. and Transport Officer will report to Orderly Room when ready to move when a time for passing the starting point will be given.

O.C.s Coys. will note the following times.

Transport packed ready to move Blankets and packs dumped

Ammunition issued up to 120 rounds arrival at starting point.

Any note of difficulties and arrangements for accelerating Operation.

Blankets and packs will be stacked in Coy. Areas for this practice.

Mess Kits will not be moved.

Rations for the following day will not be interfered with.

Reference Orders for Reserve Force move to Assembly Position.
───────────

Para 2. Line 5 :-

" " " For 1 Section R.B. read 1 Officer and 6 O. Ranks.

Para 2 Line 2:-

" " " Read " 2 Batteries R.F.A. and 1 Section Hows.

BRUEL.
20.4.19.

O.C. Crust
Lt.Colonel.
Commanding 51st. Bn. Liverpool Regiment.

DISTRIBUTION.
─────

1.- "King's Brigade.
2.- Commanding Officer.
3.- 2nd in Command.
4.- Adjutant.
5.- "
6.- " All Companies.
7.- "
8.- "
9.- Transport Officer.
10. Quartermaster.
11. Intelligence Officer.
12. R.F.A.
13. R.F.A. 168th Brigade.
14. 205th Fld Ambulance.
15. R.E. 206th Field-Coy.
16. X. Corps Cyclists.
17. Machine Gun "D" Coy.
18. File "
19. War Diary.
20. War Diary.

Reference Orders for Reserve Force to move forward.

Para 1. Read:-
"On receipt of one word Advance from Brigade H.Q. the Reserve Force etc.

Para 2. Read Line 5:-
"2 Batteries R.F.A. and 1 Section Hows."
Line 7:-
" "D" Coy less 1 Platoon".
Line 10:-
"insert 1 Platoon "D" Coy.

Para 7. Line 2:-
After PRIESTERBERG insert SEAFEN.

Para 8. :-
After American Division at GRIESENBACH LINDSCHEID line insert "and at the road junction 1½ miles S.E. of BUDENBACH on the BUDENBACH - GRIESENBACH. road.

BUCEL.
20.4.19.

A.C.Crawford
Lt. Colonel.
Commanding 51st, Bn. Liverpool Regiment.

DISTRIBUTION.
----

1. - King's Brigade.
2. - Commanding Officer.
3. - 2nd in Command.
4. - Adjutant.
5.)
6.) All Companies.
7.)
8.)
9. - Transport Officer.
10. -
11. - Intelligence Officer.
12. - R.F.A. -
13. - R.F.A - 168 th Brigade.
14. - 99th Field Ambulance.
15. - R.E. 206th Field Coy.
16. - X. Corps Cyclists.
17. - Machine Gun "D" Coy.
18. - File.
19. - War Diary.
20. - War Diary.

WAR DIARY
or
INTELLIGENCE SUMMARY

(Erase heading not required.)

Army Form C. 2118.

Place	Date	Hour	Summary of Events and Information	Remarks and references to Appendices
			Orderly Room. 51st Battalion, Liverpool Regiment. No. 1745/19 Date 31/5/19	
			# WAR DIARY. ## MAY. 1919. J. C. Powell Lieut Colonel 51 Kings Liverpool Regt	

WAR DIARY or INTELLIGENCE SUMMARY

Army Form C. 2118.

(Erase heading not required.)

Instructions regarding War Diaries and Intelligence Summaries are contained in F. S. Regs., Part II. and the Staff Manual respectively. Title Pages will be prepared in manuscript.

Place	Date	Hour	Summary of Events and Information	Remarks and references to Appendices
BEUEL	1/5/19	0800 0910	Orders received for practice POSITIONS. Coys ready to move 0950 Coys arrived Starting Point 1045 Battalion arrived Nr Holton. Orders received for Lt. Col. Watson C.M.G. D.S.O. to proceed to 51 Manchesters	16b
	2/5/19	0900 0945 1430	Platoon Training. Lt. Col. Watson proceeded to 51 Manchesters. Conference Brigade Headquarters Present C.O. Adj. & Coy Commanders. Capt Roberts & Lieut Considine interviewed by Brigadier	16b
	3/5/19	0900	Platoon Training. Capt E.G. Rathbone proceeded on leave.	16b
	4/5/19	0930	Church Parade.	16b
	5/5/19	0900 1430	Platoon Training. Conference at Brigade H.Q. Lieut S. Lee M.C. proceeded on leave. 2/Lieut. H.J. Porter proceeded to CALAIS on leave conducting duty.	16b

WAR DIARY or INTELLIGENCE SUMMARY

Place	Date	Hour	Summary of Events and Information	Remarks and references to Appendices
BEUEL	6/5/19	0900	Platoon Training	
BEUEL	7/5/19	0900	Platoon Training	Initials
BEUEL	8/5/19	0900	Platoon Training. 2/Lieut. H.J. Bowyer proceeded to CALAIS conducting Leave Party	Initials
BEUEL	9/5/19	0900	Platoon Training. Capt. & R.C.H. Buchannon proceeded to R.G.A. Goddesberg	Initials
BEUEL	10/5/19	0900	Kit Inspections & Interior Economy. 2 Lieut C.H. Willer & 1 OR proceeded for demobilize. 2/Lieut H.J. Bowyer returned from CALAIS	Initials
BEUEL	11/5/19	0930	Church Parade. 36 OR proceeded to Machine Gun Battalion. 20 OR proceeded on Transport Course at A/168 Bde. R.F.A.	Initials

WAR DIARY or INTELLIGENCE SUMMARY

Army Form C. 2118.

(Erase heading not required.)

Place	Date	Hour	Summary of Events and Information	Remarks and references to Appendices
BEUEL	12/5/19	0900	Platoon Training. Major J.O. Widdows, MC reported as 2nd in Command	16h
	13/5/19	1015	Inspection by Commander in Chief at Hangelar. Capt J.V. Addy returned from leave	16h
	14/5/19	0900	Platoon Training. 7 men proceeded for Course - Carrier Pigeons. 1 man proceeded on Divn. Education Course. 29 OR attached to R.A.S.C	16h
	15/5/19	0900	Platoon Training. 2 OR attached to X Corps Cyclists. 5 OR " to Lancs Divn Signal Cy. 29 OR " to R.A.S.C. Lieut G.S. Smith reported from England	16h
	16/5/19	0900	Lt & Q.M. S Haugh DCM took over duties of Q.M. Platoon training.	16h
	17/5/19	0900	Platoon training. 1 man proceeded to Ordination Course Cologne. 10 OR attached to 90th Field Ambulance. 27 OR attached to 206th Field Coy RE. 25 OR attached to 219 Field Coy RE. 7 OR returned from Carrier Pigeons course. Amended orders for Reserve Force issued	"A" 16h
	18/5/19		5 OR attached to 218 Field Coy RE. 8 OR attached to R.A.S.C. 2/Lieut C.T.M. HALL proceeded to conduct leave party to Calais. Church Parade	16h

WAR DIARY or INTELLIGENCE SUMMARY

Army Form C. 2118.

(Erase heading not required.)

Place	Date	Hour	Summary of Events and Information	Remarks and references to Appendices
BEUEL	18/5/19		2 O.R. Proceeded to X Corps Education Course. 36 O.R. returned from M.G. Battn. Lieut J.S. ANDERSON attached to B Coy, Machine Gun Battalion. Lieut G.S. SMITH attached to A/168 Bde R.F.A. 2/Lt H.J. PORTER attached to 1st Kings Bde T.M.B. 1 O.R. attached to Divn Signal Coy.	
	19/5/19	0830	Company Training	
	20/5/19	0730	Company Training Conference Brigade H.Q. at 1630 Commanding Officer only. Fresh Orders issued for Reserve Force to move forward Capt S Munt proceeded to Preston on duty. Lieuts C.J.W. BRYER and A.N. MARCHANT reported from England	"B"
	21/5/19	0730	Company Training Orders for Flying Patrol cancelled. Amended orders issued	"C"
	22/5/19	0730	Company Training. Capt & Q.M. W. KEATING proceeded for Demobilization.	
	23/5/19	0730	Company Training 12 O.R. attached to 565 A.T. Coy RE. 5 O.R. attached to D.D.M.S. X Corps	

WAR DIARY or INTELLIGENCE SUMMARY

Army Form C. 2118.

(Erase heading not required.)

Place	Date	Hour	Summary of Events and Information	Remarks and references to Appendices
Beuel	24/5/19	0830	Kit Inspection & Organization. Lieut F. H. KING attended 1 day Cookery Course at COLOGNE. Capt PATTINSON posted as M.O.	
	25/5/19	0930	Church Parade. Lieut J. S. ANDERSON returned from M.G.C. Lieut G. S. SMITH returned from A/168 Bde R.F.A.	
	26/5/19	0830	Company Training. Capt J. W. COOKE attached to 84 Bde R.G.A. 2/Lieut H. J. BOWYER attached to M.G.C. 2/Lieut C. E. BILLINGTON attached to A/168 Bde R.F.A.	
	27/5/19	0830	Company Training. D Coy on Ramersdorf Range. 1 O.R. attended X Corps Education Course, BONN. 11 O.R. attached to Lancs Divn Signal Coy. 1 O.R. attached Lancs Divn H.Q.	
	28/5/19	0830	Company Training. Lieut E. H. HEATH proceeded to England on leave and to attend Education Course. Secret Order No. 1 issued.	D
	29/5/19	0830	Platoon Tactical exercise for Divisional General by C. Coy. 8 O.R. attached 42nd M.V.S. 5 O.R. attached X.V.E.S.	
	30/5/19	0830	Company Training. C Coy on Ramersdorf Range. Lieut (A/Capt) H. J. RATHBONE posted to 52nd MANCHESTER Regt. Lieut H. KELLY posted to 53rd MANCHESTER Regt.	
	31/5/19	0800	Kit Inspection Interior Economy.	

SECRET

"A"

ORDERS FOR RESERVE FORCE.
~~MOVEMENT~~ ASSEMBLY POSITION.

1. On receipt of the order "POSITIONS" the Reserve Force will concentrate at the Assembly Position in and about NIEDER HOLTORF with Force H.Q. at the School at cross-roads in S.E. corner of square 17.

2. The Force will consist of:-
   51st. Bn. THE KING'S (Liverpool) REGT. from BEUEL.
   3 Platoons X Corps Cyclists from BONN.
   1 Sections "B" Coy. Machine Gun Bn. from OBERCASSEL.
   1 Section "B" Coy. Machine Gun Bn. from OBERCASSEL.
   1Section (2 Guns) 1st. King's Bde. Light T.M.B.
   C.O. Reserve Force:- Lt.Col. Barrett, C.M.G.,D.S.O.
                         (51st. Bn. The King's Regt.)

3. It is calculated that the Battalion should be concentrated at the Assembly Position within 4 hours of the receipt of "POSITIONS"

4. The following are measures will be taken by 51st. Bn. King's on receipt of orders to prepare to move:-
   (a) Packs and blankets, and other spare kit will be stacked at the theatre in BONNERSTRASSE, lately occupied by "B" Coy., and placed under a guard of 1 N.C.O. and 6 men to be detailed from surplus left behind.
   (b) All surplus Officers and O.R.'s will assemble at the Orderly Room under the Orderly Officer. The Senior Officer will take command, and report to O.C. Brigade- School, and assist in the defence of BEUEL.
        (FRIEDRICH-WILHELM HÜTTE)
   (c) All Company Transport will report at Coy. H.Q.
   (d) 4 Pack Animals & 4 Drivers will report at once to H.Q. 1st. King's Bde. Light T.M.B. to carry guns, etc.
   (e) Ammunition to complete 120 rounds per man will be issued.
   (f) The Battalion will parade in "Fighting Order", with unexpired portion of the day's rations in mess tin.
   (g) Cookers will carry oneday's rations.
   (h) Companies will report to Orderly Room when ready to move.

   Other units will conform, as far as it concerns them.

5. On the order being given to move the Battalion will march to NIEDER HOLTORF.
   Starting-point:-   200 yards E. of first house in PUTZCHEN, on the BEUEL – PUTZCHEN road.
   Order of march:-   H.Q., "A", "B", "C", "D".
                        Lewis Gun Limbers and cookers will march in rear of their respective companies.
                        Remainder of transport in rear of Battalion.
   Report Centre:-   Head of Battalion.
                        According to time of day Cookers will be making tea or a hot meal during the march.

6. Advance Brigade H.Q. will be at the School-house, ROISBERG.

7. ACKNOWLEDGE.

8. All previous orders to be cancelled.

Lieut.
51st (Grad) Bn. Liverpool Regt.

DISTRIBUTION.

1. 1st. King's Bn.
2. Commanding Officer.
3. 2nd.-in-command.
4. Adjutant.
5. "A" Coy.
6. "B" Coy.
7. "C" Coy.
8. "D" Coy.
9. H.Q. Coy.
10. T.O.
11. Q.M.
12. Intelligence Officer.
13. H.Q. 168 Bde. R.F.A.
14. 90th. Field Ambulance
15. 206th. Field Coy. R.E.
16. X Corps Cyclists
17. "B" Coy. 32nd. M.G. Battalion.
18. File.
19. War Diary.
20. War Diary.

ORDERS FOR RESERVE FORCE
TO MOVE FORWARD.

1. On receipt of word "Advance" from Brigade Headquarters the Reserve Force will move forward and occupy the ridge at UCKERALL.

2. The advance will be made by a series of bounds the first bound being to WESTERHUSEN and the high ground near SAND and WASHPOHL.

3. The Force will move off in the following order:-

   1 Coy X Corps Cyclists.
   "A" Coy.
   "B" "
   "C" "
   "D" "
   2 Coys 1st King's L.T.M.B.
   "D" Coy. less 1 Platoon
   Machine Gun Section ("E" Coy. 22nd. Bn. M.G.C.)
   1 Section R.E. (206 Field Coy.)
   1 Platoon "D" Coy.
   2 Batteries 18 pdr and 1 Section Hows. 155 Brigade R.F.A. will come under orders of O.C. Force and the Officer commanding these Batteries will report to O.C. 31st. K.L.R. for instructions at School House MIDDEN HOLTORF. The Batteries will take up positions as quickly as possible near DUPMUHL. The Batteries will cover the advance into the first objective.
   1 N.C.O. and 12 bearers of 20th. Field Ambulance will come under orders of O.C. 31st. K.L.R.

4. The Cyclists Coy. attached 31st. K.L.R. will act as vanguard to the Infantry as far as the UERATH line, getting touch with 3rd. Brigade on left about STIMMEL B. and the Americans at the road junction 12 miles S.E. of WIDERBACH on the MIDDENBACH-CHILDENBACH road. From thence it will push on either Infantry support getting touch with the Americans at ORIENBACH.
   The boundary between 1st and 3rd. Brigades will be BLAUKERBACH-WESTERHUSEN-HUCHEL-OSTERLADERO (all inclusive to 1st. Bde.)
   This will give the WESTERHUSEN-ORMPLIES road and all roads N of it for the use of the first Bde.

5. "A" "B" Coys. will move on and occupy WESTERHUSEN via STIRLDORP, BROOKHOTH, DUPMUHL, FREDEVINKEL, KLARKENHACH, WESTERHUSEN.
   "C" & "D" Coys. will move on and occupy the high ground at SAND & WASHPOHL via STIELDORF, STIELDORFHOH.
   The Machine Gun Section will support "D" Coys. and will also be responsible for the right flank of the Force.
   R.E. & R.A.M.C. will move via STIELDORFHOH to ORMPLIES when the above mentioned position is occupied.
   Signals. A Station will be established at ROTT. Report Centre will move via STIELDORFHOH, NULLINGNUSEN and ORMPLIES.

6. When this bound has been completed a halt will be made and the Batteries will move forward to cover the next bound.
   Officers will reconnoitre with a view to a further move forward which will be made by the two supporting Companies leap-frogging and will be to the area vicinity of the line MICHEL-BROICH.
   The Cyclists will move forward as soon as the Infantry are established in the WESTERHUSEN-SAND line to secure the crossing of the River HAVP.
   Report Centre will move to high ground above WILLESBERG.
   R.E. & R.A.M.C. will move from ORMPLIES along the WILLESBERG road.

(To sheet 2.)

(2.)

7. The next bound will be to the final objective viz: the UCKERATH ridge and the high ground at PRIESTERBERG, BULLESBACH & SEAFEN. Unless required in support of the leap-frogging Companies, the Companies at HUCHEL and BROICH will hold that line as a support line to the final objective. Artillery positions will probably be South of WELLESBERG. Report Centre near HOVE.
R.E. & R.A.M.C. WELLESBERG.

8. When the final objective has been reached, the leading Companies will push forward officer patrols towards the GRIESENBACH line O.C. Machine Gun Section will dispose his guns to cover the outpost line for positions near the support line.

9. All previous orders will be cancelled.

10. Acknowledge.

BEUEL.
19.5.19.

Lt. Colonel.
Commanding 51st. Bn. The King's L'pool Regt.

DISTRIBUTION.

1. 1st. King's Brigade.
2. Commanding Officer.
3. 2nd in command.
4. Adjutant.
5.)
6.) All Companies.
7.)
8.)
9. Transport Officer.
10. Quartermaster.
11. Intelligence Officer.
12. R.E.A.
13. R.F.A. 168 Brigade.
14. 90th. Field Ambulance.
15. R.E. 205 Field Coy.
16. X Corps Cyclists.
17. Machine Gun
18. File.
19. War Diary.
20. War Diary.

1. O.C. "A" Company.   7. File.
2. " "B"   "   8. War Diary.
3. " "C"   "   9. 13th. King's.
5. Commanding Officer.   10. R.S.M.
6. Transport Officer.

Reference Orders for Flying Patrol dated 13.4.19.

These are cancelled and following substituted.

3. N.C.O's and 9 O.R. of the picquet, will sleep at the Orderly Room, and the Picquet Officer at 27 BONNER STRASSE. No patrols will go out during period of duty. Picquets will dismount at Reveille.

Secret Orders issued on 14th April (a copy of which is in the Orderly Officers File in the B.O.R.) still holds good.

BEUEL.
31.5.19.

[signature]
Lieut. & A/Adjt.
51st. Bn. Liverpool Regiment.

Ref. Map 1/250,000.
Sheets 59 - 1/100,000.
Sheet 2.L.

SECRET.

51st.Bn. The King's (Liverpool Regiment.) Order No.1.
Copy No.
28.5.19.

1. (a) In the event of the Germans not signing the Peace Terms they will be given at least three days to consider, after which the Lancashire Division will advance, in rear of the leading Division (EASTERN DIVISION using the following roads:-

   i. HENNEF—WISSEN—SIEGEN.
   ii. HENNEF—WALDBROL.
   iii. SIEGBURG—NEUSTADT

   (b) American troops on right will move forward with FRANKENBERG (about 45 miles East of OLPE) as their objective, whilst VI Corps on left advance towards SOEST (twelve miles N.E. of ARNSBERG).
   (c) Ultimate objective of the Lancashire Division is the Area WISSEN-WALLMENROTH—FREUDENBERG (excl.)—OLPE (excl.)—WEGERINGHSN—MEINERZHGN—MERIENHEIDE (excl.)—MUCH (excl.) — FOSBACH (excl.); that of the Eastern Division is the Area immediately to the East of the above.

2. (a) The day on which the advance commences will be known as J day.
   (b) On J minus 1 day the Lancashire Division will concentrate in its present area and SIEGBERG and BUISDORF, and the Eastern Division close to the Western edge of the Neutral Zone.

3. (a) The Division will be formed into Groups on J minus 1 day.

   1st Brigade Group will be as follows:—
      Commanded by Brig.General. T.S. Lambert C.B., C.B., C.M.G.
      29th Brigade H.A.
      1 section Field Coy. R.E. (less 1 6" How Battery).
      1st (King's) Brigade.
      1 Machine Gun Coy.
      1 Bearer Sub Division and 1 Tent Sub Division R.A.M.C.
      1 Coy Divisional Train.

   (b) 1. Affiliated Units will come under the orders of the B.G.C. on J minus 1 day at 01.00 hours.
      11. Representatives of the above will report to Bde. H.Q. on J minus 2 days by 12.00 to receive instructions.

4. (a) The Battalion will concentrate on J minus 1 day into billets or bivouacs at BUISDORF.
   (b) Surplus kit will be dumped by Coys. at Q.M. Stores 8 Rhine Strasse on J minus 1 day at 01.00 hours.
   (c) Troops will wear Marching Order.
   (d) Ammunition will be issued up to 120 rounds per man. Men marching out will be as laid down at Conference of Sergt.Majors on Saturday last.
   (e) No blankets will be carried.

5. Orders for march will be issued later.

BEUEL,
28.5.19.

Acknowledge

Commanding 51st. Bn. The King's (L'pool Regt)

DISTRIBUTION.
----

1. Commanding Officer.
2. 2nd in Command.
3. Adjutant.
4. O.C. "A" Coy.
5. O.C. "B" "
6. O.C. "C" "
7. O.C. "D" "
8. O.C. H.Q. "
9. Intelligence Officer.
10. Transport Officer.
11. Quartermaster.
12. Files.
13. War Diary.
14. War Diary.

WAR DIARY
or
INTELLIGENCE SUMMARY

Army Form C. 2118.

(Erase heading not required.)

Instructions regarding War Diaries and Intelligence Summaries are contained in F. S. Regs., Part II. and the Staff Manual respectively. Title Pages will be prepared in manuscript.

Place	Date	Hour	Summary of Events and Information	Remarks and references to Appendices
			War Diary June 1919	

WAR DIARY or INTELLIGENCE SUMMARY

Army Form C. 2118.

(Erase heading not required.)

Place	Date	Hour	Summary of Events and Information	Remarks and references to Appendices
BEVEL	1/6/19	0930	Church Parade. 4 OR attended British Empire Leave Club. 2/Lieut H.J. BOWYER returned from M.G.C. 2/Lieut C.E. BILLINGTON returned from R.F.A.	tb
BEVEL	2/6/19	0800	Coy Training B Coy Ramersdorf Range. Lieut C.T.M. HALL attached B Coy 32nd M.G.C. 6 OR proceeded on Tradesmen Courses. 2/Lieut F.H. Nicholson attached A/168 R.F.A. 1 OR attended 1st Class Army Education Certificate Course.	tb
BEVEL	3/6/19		Kings Birthday Feu de Joie. fired. A/Capt H.J. RATHBONE returned from leave. 1 OR attended P&R.T. Course 8 OR attached Lancs Divn Signal Coy.	tb
BEVEL	4/6/19	0800	Coy Training. 7 OR attended Carrier Pigeon Course. Rev. D.W. Murray, C.F. ceased to be attached. 2/Lieut E.Y. BENFIELD posted to Eastern Divn. 250 OR proceeded on Rhine Trip.	tb
BEVEL	5/6/19	0800	Coy Training. 1 Rider to M.V.S. 1 OR attached to P.M. G.H.Q. 4 OR returned from British Empire Leave Club.	tb
BEVEL	6/6/19	0800	Coy Training. 1 OR attended Magic Lantern Course. 1 L.D Mule from D.A.C. 1 Kings Brigade Order No 2 Received with map	tb
BEVEL	7/6/19	0800	Company Training. 1 Officer attached Machine Gun Battalion 1 week 1 " " A/168 Brigade R.F.A.	tb
BEVEL	8/6/19		Church Parades	tb
Bevel	9/6/19	1000	Coy Training Lieut F.P. SCRIVEN member of F.G.C.M.	tb
	10/6/19		Coy Training. 1 Kings Brigade Instructions re advance received.	tb
		1000	Capt W.H. MORAN member of Summary Court	tb

WAR DIARY or INTELLIGENCE SUMMARY

Army Form C. 2118.

(Erase heading not required.)

Place	Date	Hour	Summary of Events and Information	Remarks and references to Appendices
BEUEL	11/6/19	0800	Coy. Training. 2 O.R. attended British Empire Leave Club. Capt. J.W. COOKE MC returned from 84 Bde R.F.A.	
	12/6/19	0800	Coy. Training	
	13/6/19	0800	Coy. Training	
	14/6/19	0800	Kit Inspections. Lieuts H.B. SPENCER, W.W. BROWN, A.R. HAYFORD, J.E. STONES, J.C. HORROCKS to UK for leave. Capt S. MUNT & Capt E.H.G. ROBERTS returned from leave	
	15/6/19		Church Parades. Capt PATTINSON returned from leave.	
	16/6/19	0800	Coy. Training. Notification received that J day will probably be June 20. & Coys advised. Lieut A.G. GRIGGS attached to A/68 Bde R.F.A – Lieut L.H. NICHOLSON attached to 3 Coy M.G.C. 1 OR attached to Lancs Divn Signals	
	17/6/19	0800	Coy. Training. Outpost Troops not to withdrawn until noon J minus 1 day. Commander in Chief's Inspection cancelled. Order No. 2 (51 KLR) issued move to Buisdorf on J day – Minus 1. Lieut F.A.R. Considine to U.K. on leave.	A
	18/6/19		Orders received for Outpost Coys to remain in position until Jump is given. Lieut G.S. SMITH member of Summary Court. Lieut A.H. GRIGGS & 2/Lt L.H. NICHOLSON returned. Capt PATTINSON R.A.M.C. ceased to be attached.	
BOISDORF	19/6/19	0852	Move to Buisdorf Arrived 11-10 hours. B2 BD at BOISDORF A & C at STOSSDORF. 51 Kings No 3 issued to Advance Guard troops	B

WAR DIARY or INTELLIGENCE SUMMARY

(Erase heading not required.)

Army Form C. 2118.

Place	Date	Hour	Summary of Events and Information	Remarks and references to Appendices
BOISDORF	20/6/19	0900	Battalion H.Q moved to STOSSDORF A & C. Coys returned to BOISDORF	
STOSSDORF	21/6/19	0900	Nothing to report. Training carried out. 2 OR attended Tradesman Course. - Lieut S. LEE discharged Hospital	
	22/6/19	0900	Nothing further to report. 2/Lieut P.W. KELLY to U.K. on leave. 1 OR attached Lancs Divn Signals	
	23/6/19		Capt S. MUNT, Lieut Nicholson & Anderson placed under close arrest. 1 OR attended Cookery Course - 4 OR to Divn Reception Camp. Lieut A.H.G. GRIGGS to U.K. on leave.	
	24/6/19	1000	Nothing to Report. Major J.A. WIDDOWS M.C. President of Summary Court - Capt W.H. MORAN to U.K. on leave	
	25/6/19		Brigade Order No 3 received in the event Peace being signed. Lieut F.P. SCRIVEN to U.K. on leave.	
	26/6/19		Nothing to report. Lieut A.J.P. HEGARTY to U.K. on leave.	
	27/6/19		Nothing to report. Lieut R.P. VENN returned from Army Reconnaissance School. Capt J.W. DUNN, CF to U.K. on leave.	
	28/6/19	1900	Notification received Peace signed by telephone	
		2305	Confirmation by wire A day will be 30 June. 4 OR attached to X.V.E.S.	

WAR DIARY or INTELLIGENCE SUMMARY

Army Form C. 2118.

Place	Date	Hour	Summary of Events and Information	Remarks and references to Appendices
STOSSDORF	29/6/19	1000	Preparations for move to Beuel. Orders issued. - Lieut E WILTSHIRE from Hospital	
	30/6/19		Move to BEUEL passed starting point 0616 arrived 0815.	
BEUEL			Remainder day in settling down in Billets. 2 OR to British Empire Leave Club.	

Appendix A

Ref Map. 1/250,000.
Sheet 59. 1/100000
Sheet 2.S.S.

SECRET

51st Bn The King's (Liverpool Regiment) Order No.2.

Copy No. 2.

17.6.19.

J day will be Friday 20th June.

On J - 1 day the Battalion will move to Zuisdorf as per 51st King's Liverpool Order No.1. Loading Company will pass the starting point, the Railway Bridge at F6.99 B25 at 0852.

Order of March:- H.Q. Company, A, B, C, D, Transport.

Dress Fighting Order.

Packs will be stacked outside 3.O.R. at 0530 on 19th and Orderly Officer will supervised loading

Rations and Water:- Remainder of days rations will be carried either on Cooker or men. Water bottles to be filled.

Iron Rations will be issued to-morrow 18th.

AMMUNITION. All ranks to be made up to 120 rounds. Any surplus to be returned to Q.M. at Surplus Kit Store on 18th.

BAGGAGE ETC. Officers valises will be at Guard Room by 0700 hours on 19.6.19.

SURPLUS KITS. Officers surplus kit, men's kit Bags and blankets and other stores, will be sent to surplus store dump at 85 30 Innerstrasse to-morrow commencing at 0630. Blankets to be rolled in tens, and securely tied and labelled by Companies. All mens Kit Bags will be labelled. Companies will be responsible for making a list of all stores sent to surplus kit store. (In duplicate)

SURPLUS PERSONNEL. All men left behind over and above this Guard mentioned above, Lieut King and Batman and Sgt Upton will parade outside B.O.R. at 0730, and will proceed 19.6.19. to Divisional Reception Camp, Wilhelm Caserne, Bonn.

Dress:- Full Marching Order, 1 Blanket and 24 Hours rations, in addition to remainder of the days rations.

Guard. "A" Company will find the N.C.O. Companies will detail 1 man to form part of the Guard.

BILLETING PARTY. Lieut J.V.Addy, 1 N.C.O. per Company,H.Q. and Transport will parade at 3.O.R. at 0700, and report to Staff Captain at Zuisdorf B43 28 at 0945. 19.6.19.

REPORTS. To Head of Battalion after leaving starting point.

BEUEL.
17.6.19.
Commanding 51st Bn The King's (Liverpool Regt)
Lt. Colonel

DISTRIBUTION :-
1. Commanding Officer.
2. 2nd-in-Command.
3. Adjutant.
4. O.C. "A" Company.
5. O.C. "B" Company.
6. O.C. "C" Company.
7. O.C. "D" Company.
8. O.C. "H.Q." Coy.
9. Intelligence Off.
10. Transport Officer.
11. Quartermaster.
12. File.
13. War Diary.
14. War Diary.

-:0:0:-

SECRET.

51ST BN. THE KING'S LIVERPOOL REGIMENT. ORDERS NO.3.

COPY.NO............

In the event of a further advance on J day being notified, and on J day will march as follows:-

The Advance Guard will be as laid down in Brigade Order No.2.

"A" Coy. 51st. K.L.R.
1 Section 206 Field Coy. R.E.
"C" Coy. 51st. K.L.R.
1 Section "B" Coy. L.T.M.B.
"B" & "D" Coys. 51st. K.L.R.

Advance will be to the vicinity of ALZENBACH. Route HEINNEF and MERTON.

The starting point will be "A" Coys. Billet in STOBDORF:-
5. G. 30 - 10.

Order to move will be as follows:-

Jump (date) aaa (hour).

which will be time of passing starting point.

Distances on the march will be as laid down in Notes on March Discipline Type B.

Packs and Officers Valises will be stacked at Q.M. Stores
(for 51st. King's and L.T.M.B. only.)

BUISDORF.
19.6.19.

(Sgd). H. DRAKEFORD.
Lieut. A/Adjt.
Liverpool Regiment.

DISTRIBUTION.

1. "A" Coy.
2. "B" "
3. "C" "
4. "D" "
5. Medical Officer.
6. Signalling Officer.
7. Transport Officer.
8. Quartermaster.
9. Section 206 Field Coy R.E.
10. Section "B" Coy. 32. M.G.Bn.
11. Section 1st. King's. L.T.M.B.
12. War Diary.
13. War Diary.
14. File.

Appx 6

THE KING'S (LIVERPOOL) REGT.

BATTN. ORDERS No. 2.   Copy No........

1/25390.
29.6.19.

The Battalion and 1 Section King's L.T.M.B. will move back to original billeting areas on 30th June 1919.

Order of March.

A.Q.M. }
"C" Coy. }
"D" " }   6 at King's.
"A" " }
"B" " }
Transport.
1 Section King's L.T.M.B.

Section K.G. Bn. will move independently as per orders issued.

Leading Coy. will pass the starting point H.20 d.55 junction road and railway at BAISIEUX and HINGETTE road at 0600 hours. Distance between units will be maintained in accordance with "Notes on March Discipline".

"C" Coy. will detail an officer to bring along stragglers.

Regtl. Police will report to him.

Coys. and affiliated units will render a certificate that billets have been left in clean and sanitary condition.

Cooks and small billeting will be sent in advance to prepare breakfast. Necessary cooking utensils to be sent on lorry lorry.

Reveille 0430 hours. Tea and Biscuits 0500. Breakfast on arrival at BETHUNE.

29.6.19. H.Q. at NEUVE CHAPELLE.
2 new Coy. will proceed with lorries and be responsible for each cookery.

Officers valises:- O.C. Wagon will collect officers valises at 1800 hours 29.6.19. Coys. will send 1 Batman to guide Wagons and see valises are Hack on M.T. at 0500 hours 30.6.19.

Artillery will revert to the command of their own C.O's. on arrival in billeting areas.

Coys. will clear stores from 65 BONANGERION immediately after breakfast 30.6.19.

ACKNOWLEDGE.

DIRECTION.
As per Bgd. Orders No.2. less 1 Section Rd Coy. R.E.

SUMMARY.
29.6.19.

                              C.Wakefym
                              Capt. Adjt.
                              2nd. Bn. Liverpool Regiment.

MESSAGE FORM.

Army Form C 2128.

TO Infantry Rec

FROM & Place S Kings

Originator's Number 6401

Day of Month 4

In reply to Number G 85

original copy forwarded to Records Preston duplicate is returned herewith

Time of Handing In 4/10

Originator's Signature W Walker Capt

MESSAGE FORM.

Army Form C 2128
(pads of 100)

CALL	In	Recd. At ___ By ___
	Out	Sent At ___ By ___

PREAMBLE:

M.M. } Delivery
Offices (Origin

Date Stamp

TO | 51st Kings & /oo?/ Regt

PREFIX ___ Words ___ v ___

FROM & Place: **G.O.C.**

Originator's Number: **1st Bde.**

Day of Month: **3**

In reply to Number:

Attached draw[?] for work of duplicate copy. Please forward original copy to reach this office not later than 1700 hrs tomorrow 4.

TIME OF ORIGIN

TIME OF HANDING IN
(For Signal use only)

Originator's Signature
(Not Telegraphed): Major [illegible]

WAR DIARY
or
INTELLIGENCE SUMMARY.

Army Form C. 2118.

(Erase heading not required.)

Place	Date	Hour	Summary of Events and Information	Remarks and references to Appendices
			War Diary	
			July 1919.	
			J.O. Widdows Major. o.c 51st Kings Liverpool Regt	

WAR DIARY or INTELLIGENCE SUMMARY.

Army Form C. 2118.

Instructions regarding War Diaries and Intelligence Summaries are contained in F. S. Regs., Part II. and the Staff Manual respectively. Title pages will be prepared in manuscript.

(Erase heading not required.)

Place	Date	Hour	Summary of Events and Information	Remarks and references to Appendices
BEVEL	1.7.19	0900	Issue of Web Equipment to Coys. 7 OR attached Lanes Div. Train. 1 OR attached 61 S.S. 4 OR attended Education Course	
	2.7.19		Brigade Rifle Competition. Lieuts W W BROWN A R HAYFORD J E STONES J C HORROCKS H B SPENCER returned from Leave.	
	3.7.19		Bde Rifle Compn and Holiday commemorating signing of Peace. Lieut F A R. CONSIDINE returned from Leave	
	4.7.19		Bde Rifle Competition	
	5.7.19		Kit Inspection	
	6.7.19		Church Parade Special Service of Thanksgiving. 4 OR to Leave Club. 5 OR visit Battle area - YPRES. Capt J N COOK.G + 4 OR proceed to PARIS for Victory March	
	7.7.19		Practice Khud Race - Col. OE CORBETT, 2 L/GM G HAIGH + 2 OR to PARIS for Victory March	
	8.7.19		Practice Khud Race - 1 OR to Army Dental Centre	

WAR DIARY
or
INTELLIGENCE SUMMARY.
(Erase heading not required.)

Army Form C. 2118.

Instructions regarding War Diaries and Intelligence Summaries are contained in F. S. Regs., Part II. and the Staff Manual respectively. Title pages will be prepared in manuscript.

Place	Date	Hour	Summary of Events and Information	Remarks and references to Appendices
BEVEL	9.7.19	1400	Bde Boxing Competition — Lieut A.H.G. GRIGGS } returned from leave. 2/Lieut W KELLY }	
BEVEL	10.7.19			
BEVEL	11.7.19		Lieut F P SCRIVEN returned from leave.	
BEVEL	12.7.19		1 OR to Army School of Musketry — Lieut J E STONES and 1 OR to Ordination Course. Lieut A J P HEGNEY returned from leave	
BEVEL	13.7.19		Church Parade	
BEVEL	14.7.19		2/Lieut H J BOWYER returned from leave. VICTORY MARCH - PARIS.	
BEVEL	15.7.19		Capt E.H.G. ROBERTS MC and Lieut S LEE MC members of Summary Court. Capt. W.T.G. MOFFAT CF attached.	
BEVEL	16.7.19		2 OR to British Empire Leave Club — 4 OR to Lancs Divn Signal Coy RE. 250 OR proceed on Rhine Trip. Lieut J.H.M LITTLE MC returned from BIRKHAMPSTEAD	

WAR DIARY or INTELLIGENCE SUMMARY.

Army Form C. 2118.

(Erase heading not required.)

Place	Date	Hour	Summary of Events and Information	Remarks and references to Appendices
BEUEL	17/7/19		56 OR to UK demob and re-enlistment furlough	
BEUEL	18/7/19			
BEUEL	19/7/19			
BEUEL	20/7/19		CHURCH PARADE. - RSM JONES returned from U.K.	
BEUEL	21/7/19		Capt. E.H.G. ROBERTS member of F.G.C.M. - Lieut C.T.M. HALL attached A/168 Bde R.F.A. Lieut J.H. LOWEN attached M.G.C.	
BEUEL	22/7/19		2/Lt N.H. BUTTS to UK on leave.	
BEUEL	23/7/19		2/Lt H.T. PORTER to U.K. on leave - Brigade Competition. Sports. Lieut E.H. HEATH returned from course.	
BEUEL	24/7/19		British War Medal Riband issued.	

WAR DIARY
or
INTELLIGENCE SUMMARY.

(Erase heading not required.)

Army Form C. 2118.

Place	Date	Hour	Summary of Events and Information	Remarks and references to Appendices
BEUEL	25.7.19			
BEUEL	26.7.19		2 OR attended British Empire Leave Club - Lieut C.T.M. HALL returned from A/168 Bde R.F.A. Lieut J.H.L. OWEN returned from M.G.C. - Lieut E. WILTSHIRE to U.K. for leave.	
BEUEL	27.7.19		Lieut H. BUSH returned from Hospital	
BEUEL	28.7.19		Bad weather. Inspection of Animal accounts by D.V.C.	
BEUEL	29.7.19		A. & C. Coys G.R.C. at Ramersdorf - 4 OR to UK leave.	
BEUEL	30.7.19		Lieut C.J.W. BRYER member of Summary Court - Lieut H.B. SPENCER attached Lancs Divn Train. Capt J.VADDY MC attended Cookery Demonstration. 4 OR to U.K. leave - Capt J.W. COOKE and Lieut J.H.M. LITTLE members of F.G.C.M.	
BEUEL	31.7.19		4 OR to U.K. leave. 1 OR to UK for re-enlistment furlough	

51st Battalion The King's (Liverpool) Regiment

WAR DIARY

August 1919.

O. C. Donald
Colonel
Comdg. 51st Bn The King's (Liverpool) Regt.

WAR DIARY or INTELLIGENCE SUMMARY.

(Erase heading not required.)

Army Form C. 2118.

Place	Date	Hour	Summary of Events and Information	Remarks and references to Appendices
BEUEL	1/8/19		Operation Order No 5 issued. Major J.O. WIDDOWS to UK Leave. Capt. Roberts M.C. assumed command	A
		1800	Orders received cancelling relief of Outposts	
	2/8/19	2200	Order received. Eastern Division proceeding to England.	
		10.30	Adjt proceeded with BGC to see new line	
		1500	Orders received cancelling all previous instructions re Eastern Division. Col O.C. BORRETT returned from leave and assumed command. Capt. Roberts M.C. returned to 'C' Coy.	
	3/8/19		2 OR attended Loop Set Course.	
			Order No 6 issued	B
STOSSDORF	4/8/19		Bn Moved to STOSSDORF	War B
	5/8/19		4 OR to British Empire Leave Club - Col. O.C. BORRETT & Capt J.W. COOK President and members of Summary Court. Col. O.C. BORRETT, CMG, DSO, ADC assumed command of 1st Kings Bde. Capt J.B. LEIGH R.A.M.C. attached	War B
	6/8/19		Lieut K.D.B. POCKLINGTON to UK leave	War B

WAR DIARY or INTELLIGENCE SUMMARY.

Army Form C. 2118.

Place	Date	Hour	Summary of Events and Information	Remarks and references to Appendices
STOSSDORF	7/8/19			
	8/8/19		Lieut C.T.M. HALL to U.K. on leave - 2/Lieut W.H. CUTTS returned from leave. Capt J.E. BRIDGE R.A.M.C. attached. Capt W.I.G. MOFFAT, C.F. attached - Capt J.B. LEIGH R.A.M.C. returned to 13th K.L.R.	
	9/8/19			
	10/8/19		1 O.R. attended Lance Down Education Course. Col. O.C. BORRETT, C.M.G., D.S.O., A.D.C. relinquished Command of 1st Kings Bde.	
	11/8/19		4 O.R. attended Courses for Apprentice Tradesmen. 2/Lieut H.J. BOWYER attached to A/168 Bde R.F.A. - Lieut F.A.R. CONSIDINE returned from A/168 Bde R.F.A. Lieut E.H. HEATH returned from leave.	

WAR DIARY or INTELLIGENCE SUMMARY.

Army Form C. 2118.

(Erase heading not required.)

Place	Date	Hour	Summary of Events and Information	Remarks and references to Appendices
STOSSDORF	12/8/19		3 OR attended Cookery Course COLOGNE. 2 OR attended Class for 1st class Education Certificate. 2/Lieut H.J. PORTER returned from leave.	
	13/8/19		Lieuts F.A.R. CONSIDINE and C.J.W. BRYER proceeded for duty with Directors of Graves Registration. Lieut S LEE MC. to UK leave. Capt & Adjt H DRAKEFORD MC to UK leave. Lieut E WILTSHIRE returned from leave.	
	14/8/19			
	15/8/19		2 OR. to British Empire Leave Club	
	16/8/19		1 OR to Army School of Musketry DROVE. "C" Coy. moved from BUISDORF to STIELDORF in relief of a Coy. of 13th Kings. Arrangements made between Coy Commanders concerned.	

WAR DIARY or INTELLIGENCE SUMMARY

Army Form C. 2118.

Place	Date	Hour	Summary of Events and Information	Remarks and references to Appendices
STOSSDORF	17/8/19		Lieut J.H.L.OWEN to U.K. leave — Rev. F. MORRISSEY C.F. attached. 2/Lieut H.J. BOWYER returned from A/168 Bde R.F.A.	
	18/8/19		Extract from G.H.Q. List No 14 received — Appointment of Lieuts J.V. ADDY, MC and J.W. COOK MC to A/Capt. whilst commanding Coys — 2/Lt J.S. ANDERSON att. A/168 R.F.A	
	19/8/19			
	20/8/19		"B" & "C" Coys. Musketry Part III G.M.C. DAMBROICH.	
	21/8/19		Lieut F.P. SCRIVEN to U.K. for duty with Cost Accounting Committee. Lieut G. HAIGH to U.K. leave	

WAR DIARY or INTELLIGENCE SUMMARY.

Army Form C. 2118.

(Erase heading not required.)

Instructions regarding War Diaries and Intelligence Summaries are contained in F. S. Regs., Part II. and the Staff Manual respectively. Title pages will be prepared in manuscript.

Place	Date	Hour	Summary of Events and Information	Remarks and references to Appendices
	27/8/19		6 OR. leave to UK.	A&B
			"A" & "D" Coys Dambroich Range.	A&B
	28/8/19		Lieut S. Munt proceeded for duty w. 52nd Welsh Regt. on struck off strength	A&B
			6 OR leave to U.K. B & "C" Coys DAMBROICH Range.	
			1st. Kings Bde G 10/2/9 re move to BONN received.	
	29/8/19		Capt. H. Drakeford M.C. returned from leave to U.K.	A&B
			Lieut J.A.M. Little M.C. admitted hospital.	
			6 O.R. leave to UK. Operation Order No 7 published.	C
	30/8/19		3 OR attend Tradesman Course SIEGBURG. 6 OR. leave to UK.	A&B
			"C" Coy Musketry DAMBROICH.	
	31/8/19		6 OR leave to UK	A&B

WAR DIARY or INTELLIGENCE SUMMARY.

Army Form C. 2118.

(Erase heading not required.)

Place	Date	Hour	Summary of Events and Information	Remarks and references to Appendices
	22/8/19		1 O.R. to Graves Registration & Enquiries, FRANCE.	W.W.B
			MAJOR J.O. WIDDOWS M.C. returned from leave	
	23/8/19		8 O.R. attend 1st King's Bde Class of Instruction. Retreat 1900 hrs. till further orders.	W.W.B
			Lieut R.J. VENN to U.K. leave. - 6 O.R. to U.K. leave	
			Lieut H.D.B. Pocklington returned leave.	
	24/8/19		1 O.R. to P. & R.T. School RIEHL. - 2 O.R. to British Empire Leave Club	W.W.B
			6 O.R. to U.K. leave	
	25/8/19		2/Lt J.S. ANDERSON att. Lancs Dvn Team	W.W.B
			6 O.R. to U.K. leave 'A' & 'D' Coys DAMBROICH Range.	
	26/8/19		6 O.R. to U.K. leave. 'B' & 'C' Coys. DAMBROICH Range.	W.W.B

Ref Sheets BONN & SIEGBURG 1/25,000.

SECRET   Copy No........

51st. KING'S LIVERPOOL REGIMENT ORDER No. 5.

1. "D" Coy 51st. K.L.R. will relieve the Coy of 13th.K.L.R. on Control Posts in the left Sector of the Brigade front on 2.8.19. On relief Coy. 13th. K.L.R. will take over billets of "D" Coy. 51st. K.L.R.

2. (a) All information with regard to the outpost line and control posts and all training facilities in the area will be taken over.

   (b) All defence schemes will be taken over.

3. "D" Coy. 51st. K.L.R. will move off from Billets at 0800 hours. Field Kitchen and Lewis Gun Limber will proceed and remain with Coy.

4. Motor Lorry will report at 0830 hours to carry mens kit bags and surplus stores.

5. Advance party of 1 officer and 4 N.C.O's will proceed on 1st. August to take over billets etc.

6. Signalling Officer will make necessary arrangements with S.O. of 13th. King's for telephone communication.

7. Marching out state and list of men remaining with Battalion will be sent to B.O.R. by 1700 hours on 1st. August.

8. Billets will be left in a clean and sanitary condition and certificate sent to B.O.R.

9. Completion of relief will be wired to Battalion H.Q.

10. "D" Coy. will acknowledge.

BEUEL
31.7.19.

(signature)
Capt. & Adjt.
51st. Battalion King's Liverpool Regiment.

Issued at ....

DISTRIBUTION.

Copy No. 1. War Diary.
2.   "
3. File.
4. O.O.
5. Adjutant.
6. 13th.K.L.R.
7. Quartermaster.
8. Signalling Officer.
9. Transport Officer.
10. Lieut. Horrocks (Billeting Offr)
11. O.C. "A" Coy.
12. O.C. "B" Coy.
13. O.C. "C" Coy.
14. O.C. "D" Coy.

SECRET.

51ST. BN. THE KING'S LIVERPOOL REGIMENT. ORDER NO. 6.

Copy No.

Date. 5.8.19.

Ref Sheet.
BONN &
SIEGBURG } 1/25,000.

1. 51st. K.L.R. will take over the 1&th Battalion Sector of the 2nd Divisional Front at present occupied by the 52nd. Manchester Regt. on August 4th 1919.

2. On completion of move the Battalion will located as follows :-

   Battn. H.Q.   SNOSSERD.
   "A" & "C" Coys.   BUISDORF.
   "B"   "   ROTT.
   "D"   "   WARTH.

Move to be completed by 1700 hours.

3. All Defence Schemes, Maps etc. will be taken over, and receipts given.

4. "B" & "D" Coys will move at 0900 hours under Coy. arrangements, taking over Control posts by Advance Parties as detailed below. Remainder of Battalion will Parade at 1400 hours. Head of column to be at Bridge R. 7082. Order of March :- H.Q. "C" Coy. "A" Coy. Transport. Dress for March :- /Fighting Order".

5. Advance Parties will be detailed as follows :-
   "B" & "D" Coys. 1 Officer 2 N.C.O's. and 6 O.R's. to take over Control Posts Proceeding at 0630 hours.
   All Coys. Billeting Parties of 1 Officer and 4 O.R's. parading at B.O.R. at 0830 hours.
   "A" & "C" Coys. will billet under instructions of Lt. Horrocks.

6. Baggage and Stores.
   Coy. dumps will be made of all kits, Officers valises, Packs etc by 0800 hours, and wooden beds, tables, and forms not being taken will be dumped as follows :-

   "A" Coy.)
   "D" "   ) At Q.M. Stores.
   "B" "   )
   "C" "   )

   Palliasses will be emptied and returned to Q.M. Stores by 0730 hours. The straw will be burnt. If necessary an extra blanket will be issued from H.Q. SNOSSDORF on arrival.
   The Quartermaster will supply lorries on the second journey for the following

   1. Reg'l. Canteen.
   2. "   Cinema and Sports Gear.
   3. B.O.R. and P.R.I. Boxes.
   4. Pioneers Shop and workshops.

   Remaining departments will stack all stores at Q.M. stores by 0800 hours.

7. Loading and Rear Parties.
   (a) O.C. "A" Coy. will detail the following :-
       1 Sgt. to report at Q.M. Stores at 0700 to superintend lorries.
       1. N.C.O. and 6 men to report Q.M. Stores at 0700 as loading Party
   These men will carry remainder of the days rations.
       1 N.C.O. and 12 men to report to R.S.M. at 0730 hours.
   (b) O.C. "C" Coy. will detail 2 N.C.O.'s and 12 men under Lt. G.S. Smith to remain behind to hand over all billets etc to Town Major and obtain cleanliness certificate. Q.M. will arrange their rations for the following day.

(2)

(a) O's.C. "B" & "D" Coys. on Marching out at 0900 hours. will leave a party of 1 N.C.O. and 6 men to load lorries and clear up billets. these parties will follow later independently, reporting before departure to Lt. C.S. Smith.

6. **Meals and Rations.**

Reveille and Breakfast under Coy. arrangements.
Dinner of "A" Coy. "C" Coy. and H.Q. will be 1200 hours.
Tea on arrival.
Rations for Tuesday will be issued at SNOSSDNT on arrival.

9. All men proceeding independently i.e. with lorries etc. will wear proper equipment and carry arms.

10. Completion of moves will be reported to Battalion. H.Q.

11. Acknowledge.

BEUEL.

51st. Bn. The King's Liverpool Regt.

[signature]
Capt & Adjt.

DISTRIBUTION.

1. War Diary.   9. O.C. "D" Coy.
2. do.   10. H.Q. Coy.
3. file.   11. Transport Officer.
4. O.C.   12. Quartermaster.
5. Adjutant.   13. H.Q. 52nd. Manchester Regt.
6. O.C. "A" Coy.   14. 1st King's Bde. H.Q.
7. "B" "   15. R.S.M.
8. "C" "   16. Town Major. BEUEL.

SECRET.   Copy No.

51st. Bn. THE KING'S (LIVERPOOL) REGIMENT.

ORDER NO. 7.

In connection with the forthcoming move to BONN, an advance party, composed as under, will proceed to BONN tomorrow:
H.Q.   A.A.L.G. Section.
Sgt. Hammond.

They will report by 11.00 hours to Major J.O. Widdows, M.C. at the H.Q. 15th. Lancashire Fusiliers, in the Museum Strasse, BONN. Rations for the day will be taken. Rations for Sunday, Monday and Tuesday will be sent to them daily. T.O. will arrange conveyance of Kit Bags and blankets, which will be ready for collection at "A" Coy. Office by 08.30 hours tomorrow.

GODESBURG.
29/8/19.

Lieut. A/Adjt.
51st. Bn. The King's (Liverpool) Regt.

DISTRIBUTION.

1. C.O.   6. Q.M.
2. Adjt.   7. T.O.
3. 1st. King's Brigade. 8. War Diary.
4. O.C. A Coy.   9. File.
5. Sgt. Hammond.

CONFIDENTIAL.

WAR DIARY

51st. Bn. "The King's" (Liverpool) Regt.

Period 1-30 Sept.

1919

J.O Widdows Major.
Comdg. 51st. Bn. "The King's" (L'pool.) Regt.

BONN
30-9-19

WAR DIARY
or
INTELLIGENCE SUMMARY.
(Erase heading not required.)

Army Form C. 2118.

Instructions regarding War Diaries and Intelligence Summaries are contained in F. S. Regs., Part II. and the Staff Manual respectively. Title pages will be prepared in manuscript.

Place	Date	Hour	Summary of Events and Information	Remarks and references to Appendices
STOSSDORF	1.9.19		6 OR's leave to U.K - CAPT. J.V. ADDY. M.C. Demobilized Struck off Strength	WWB
	2.9.19		CAPT H DRANEFORD M.C. to 1st Kings Bde whilst acting Brigade Major — 8 OR's leave to U.K. Battalion moved into BONN, relieving 15th Lancs. Fusiliers.	"A" WWB
	3.9.19		COL. O.C BORRETT. C.M.G. D.S.O. A.D.C to England on duty — LIEUT. J.H.Z. OWEN returned leave to U.K. — 8 OR's leave to U.K - MAJ. J.O. WADDOWS. assumed Comdg of Bn - CAPT H. DRANEFORD. M.C assumed 2-in-C of Bn. — LIEUT. W.W. BROWN assumed the Duties Adjutant. —	WWB
	4.9.19		2 ORs to British Empire Leave Club — 8 OR's leave to U.K	WWB
	5.9.19		12 OR's leave to U.K	WWB

WAR DIARY
or
INTELLIGENCE SUMMARY.
(Erase heading not required.)

Army Form C. 2118.

Instructions regarding War Diaries and Intelligence Summaries are contained in F. S. Regs., Part II. and the Staff Manual respectively. Title pages will be prepared in manuscript.

Place	Date	Hour	Summary of Events and Information	Remarks and references to Appendices
BONN	6.9.19		6 ORs to Course at Army Science College – 1 OR to Course at Army General & Commercial College. LIEUT G. HAIGH DCM returned leave U.K. – 12 OR's leave to U.K.	WUB
	7.9.19		9 OR's to Course at Xth Corps School of Education – CAPT A.N. MARCHANT leave to U.K. –	WUB
	8.9.19		12 OR's leave to U.K. – Lt. J.H.M. LITTLE MC Discharged Hospital	WUB
	9.9.19		2 OR's to British Empire Leave Club – 12 OR's leave to U.K.	WUB
	10.9.19		LIEUT E.H. HEATH to U.K. for Demobilization – 12 OR's leave to U.K. – LIEUT NORTH taken on Strength as Education Officer – Battalion took over Town Duties etc. in BONN from 12th L.N. LANCS. REGT.	WUB

WAR DIARY or INTELLIGENCE SUMMARY.

Army Form C. 2118.

(Erase heading not required.)

Place	Date	Hour	Summary of Events and Information	Remarks and references to Appendices
BONN	11.9.19		Lieut. R.J. VENN returned leave U.K. - CAPT. J.W. COOKE M.C. returned leave UK - 4 OR's leave to U.K. - Lt. E WILTSHIRE assumed command of D Coy.	
	12.9.19		Lieut. W.M. SNELL leave to U.K. - 4 OR's leave to U.K.	
	13.9.19		8 O.R's leave to U.K.	
	14.9.19		2 OR's to British Empire Leave Club - 2/Lt. L H NICHOLSON returned leave U.K. - Lt. G.S. SMITH returned leave U.K.	
	15.9.19		8 O.R's leave to U.K.	

WAR DIARY or INTELLIGENCE SUMMARY.

Army Form C. 2118.

(Erase heading not required.)

Place	Date	Hour	Summary of Events and Information	Remarks and references to Appendices
BONN	16.9.19		8 OR's Leave U.K.	AWB
	17.9.19		11 OR's Leave U.K.	AWB
	18.9.19		9 OR's Leave U.K.	AWB
	19.9.19		2 OR's to British Empire Leave Club. 2/LT C.E. BILLINGTON Leave to U.K. — MAJOR H.S. LEWIS D.A.Y. Struck off Strength from 27.4.19 — CAPT W.H. MORAN S.O.S. from 25.6.19 — LIEUT F.A.R. GINSDIKE and LIEUT C.J.W. BRYER Struck off Strength from 13.8.19. — 10 OR's Leave U.K.	AWB
	20.9.19		4 OR's Leave U.K.	AWB

WAR DIARY or INTELLIGENCE SUMMARY.

Army Form C. 2118.

(Erase heading not required.)

Instructions regarding War Diaries and Intelligence Summaries are contained in F. S. Regs., Part II. and the Staff Manual respectively. Title pages will be prepared in manuscript.

Place	Date	Hour	Summary of Events and Information	Remarks and references to Appendices
BONN	21.9.19		1. O.R to Course at P+R.T School - CAPT H. DRAKEFORD M.C returned from Duty with 1st Kings Bn.	WWB.
	22.9.19		LIEUT G.H TOMMIS Struck off Strength from 19.4.19 - LIEUT H.A. PARRY Struck off Strength from 12.4.19. - 4 O.R's Leave U.K 2/LT. J. ROBERTS. Leave to U.K -	WWB.
	23.9.19		4 OR'S Leave UK -	WWB
	24.9.19		4 OR's Leave U.K - 2/LT H.J PORTER returned from 1st Kings I.T.M.B. - CAPT A.N. MARCHANT. returned leave U.K. -	WWB
	25.9.19		4 OR's Leave UK.	WWB.

WAR DIARY
or
INTELLIGENCE SUMMARY.
(*Erase heading not required.*)

Army Form C. 2118.

Place	Date	Hour	Summary of Events and Information	Remarks and references to Appendices
BONN.	26.9.19		4 OR's Leave to U.K. — Fire in Barracks at 2115 hrs. Report attached.	"C" W.W.B.
	27.9.19			W.W.B.
	28.9.19			W.W.B.
	29.9.19		2 OR's British Empire Leave Club —	W.W.B.
	30.9.19			W.W.B.

SECRET.

51st Bn. The King's Liverpool Regiment.

OPERATION ORDER NO. 6.

COPY NO. 18

1. In accordance with 1st King's Brigade No. G 10/2/9 the present B.ttalion Area will be handed over to the 3rd. Lancaster-Frigade and the Battalion will move into the Kaserne COBLENZER STRASSE BONN on Tuesday 2.9.19.

2. "D" Coy. will be relieved by a Coy of 53rd. Lancaster Regt. "B" & "C" Coys. less the post at SIEDORFERHOHN, will be relieved by 52nd. Lancaster Regt.
The post at SIEDORFERHOHN will be relieved by troops of 52nd. King's Liverpool Regt.
Orders re handing over of "D" Coy. to hand over and to take charge of rear party.

3. Company Commanders will march independently to new billets, starting from present area by 0800 hours.
They will leave a small rear party to load their lorry and to hand over Camp. Posts will remain as at present until relieved and will march to new billets with the rear parties. An officer will be left by each Coy. to hand over and to take charge of rear party.

4. Latrines and ablution benches will be handed over to relieving troops. Orders re tables and forms will be issued later.

5. Receipts will be obtained for all tentage and stores handed over.

6. Dinners will be cooked on the march and will be served on arrival. "B" Coy. will send their cooks to BONN on their first lorry, with rations, and dinner will be prepared for them in BONN.

7. Lorries will be available tomorrow to do one journey for each Coy. and will report about 1400 hours. Coys. will arrange to send in on this their Kit Bags and Coy Stores. Valises and blankets will be retained until Tuesday.

8. Coy. Officers Messes will detail their less useful waiters to proceed to BONN and report at the MUSEUM to Lt. Lorroches by 1900 hours. "D" Coy. will also send their cooks. There will be a Battalion Officers Mess in BONN and lunch will be served on arrival.

9. Coys. including H.Q. will render a "Marching Out Scheme" to B.O.R. by 0900 hours on Tuesday.

10. Company for duty on Tuesday will be "B" Coy. and on Wednesday "D" Coy.

11. B.O.R. will close at SIEGSDORF at 1000 hours Tuesday and will open at BONN on arrival.

12. Coys. will report move complete to B.O.R. BONN.

13. ACKNOWLEDGE.

51st. Bn. The King's Liverpool Regiment.

Lieut. & Adjt.

(1)

DISTRIBUTION.
----

1. G.O.
2. Major J.O. Widdows. M.C.
3. Adjutant.
4. O.C. "A" Coy.
5. " "B" "
6. " "C" "
7. " "D" "
8. Transport Officer.
9. Quartermaster.
10. Medical Officer.
11. R.S.M.
12. 1st. King's Brigade.
13. 52nd. King's L'pool Regt.
14. 52nd, Manchester Regt.
15. 53rd, Manchester Regt.
16. File.
17. War Diary;
18. War Diary.

---------oOo---------

B.

GUARDS FOUND BY 51st. BN. THE KING'S LIVERPOOL REGIMENT.

Serial Number	Composition	Location and duties	Under orders of	Where billeted	Remarks
1.	2 Sergeants. 4 Corporals. 18 Privates. 1 Bugler.	Corps Commander's Guard.		Corps H.Q.	Relieved weekly. Temporarily discontinued during absence of Corps Commander. Rationed away from Battn.
2.	1 Sergeant 2 Corporals 2 Buglers. 18 Privates.	Divisional Commander's Guard.		Divn. H.Q.	Remains for fortnight. Rationed away from Battalion.
3.	1 N.C.O. 6 men.	Army General Hospital escort. Larry Park Endenicher Allee.			Night Guard Mounts daily at 18.00 hours. Rationed by Battalion.
4.	3 N.C.O's. 18 men.	Guard over Goods Station BONN.	R.T.O.	Goods Station.	Relieved fortnightly. Rationed by Battalion. A cook should be attached.
5.	1 N.CO. 3 men.	47th. General Hospital escort.			Rationed away from Battn. Remain on duty fortnight.
6.	1 Officer	29th. C.C.S. escort.			Relieved daily. Washing Kit only necessary.
7.	1 Company.	Piequets BONN.	Area Commandant BONN.	Am Hof. University Buildings Officers in Hôtel Goldenenstern. Market Place.	Strength not to fall below 3 Officers and 80 O. Rs. Rationed by Battn.
8.	1 Officer.	Brigade Field Officer of the week.			
9.	The playing of "RETREAT" on the Kaiser Platz, BONN, on Sundays, also devolves upon the Unit finding the duties in BONN.				

BONN
19.9.19

1st. King's Brigade.

At about 2110 hours last night Pte. Hogg of the Unit under my Command, noticed a light in the basement of the museum. Thinking this unusual, he informed the Commander of the Quarter Guard.

On investigation he found that there was a fire in the basement. The alarm was sounded, the fire picquet stood to and the whole Battalion got to work with fire buckets, etc. Brigade, Division and Corps, H.Q. were informed and the BONN town Fire Brigade was summoned.

The latter arrived about 2140 hours. By 2230 hours the fire was well under control and it was completely extinguished by 2315 hours.

There is a large quantity of wood wool in the basement concerned and there are a number of apertures, through which a spark or lighted cigarette end might have fallen.

So far as can be ascertained no civilian whatever was seen at any time during the evening near the scene of the fire.

Beyond the burning of about half the wood wool no further damage appears to havebeen done.

B O N N.
27/9/19.

J. Chisholm.
Major,
Comdg. 51st. Bn. The King's (Liverpool) Regt.

War Diary

51st. Bn. "The King's" (Liverpool) Regt.

Period: October 1919

J O Widdows, Lieut. Col.
Comdg. 51st. Bn. "The King's" Regt.

1/11/19

SECRET.

51st. BN. THE KING'S LIVERPOOL REGIMENT
OPERATION ORDER.
BY
LIEUT. COLONEL J.O. "WIDDOWS," M.B.
BONN. 16/10/19.

1. In accordance with 1st. King's Brigade O.O. 10/2/13 of 14/10/19, the 51st. Bn. "The King's" Liverpool Regt., will take over to-morrow the area at present occupied by 52nd. King's Liverpool Regt.

2. "A" Coy. 51st. Bn. The King's Liverpool Regt., will relieve "A" Coy. 52nd. King's.
   Coy. HQ. at VINXEL.
   "B" Coy. 51st. King's, will relieve "D" Coy. 52nd. King's.
   Coy. H.Q. ROMLINGHOVEN.
   "D" Coy. 51st. King's, will take over billets etc. from "B" and "C" Coy. 52nd. King's.

3. Arrangements for relief of posts etc. have been made by Coy. Commanders concerned.

4. Stores, Baggage, etc., will be dealt with as per preliminary instructions already issued.

5. Q.M. will obtain a certificate that Barracks, etc. have been handed in a clean and sanitary condition.

6. Requisitioned Stores will be handed over "in situ". Officers i/c. Institutes and O.C. Coys. will carefully check all stores taken over and will send copies of receipts given by them, to B.O.R. by 09.00 hours 19th. inst.

7. The Q.M. and O.C. Coys., will arrange for cooks to proceed to the new area in time to prepare dinners.

8. "A" & "B" Coys. will parade complete, ready to move off at 08.00 hours, leaving a small party under an Officer N.C.O. to take charge of their lorries.
   Dress :- Marching Order. Steel Helmets carried on Valise.

9. "D" Coy. (less Bonn Guards) will form loading party and Baggage Guard and will accompany last lorries to the new area.
   H.Q. Coy. will parade under CSM. MC. Carten, at 09.00 hours and will march with transport to New Area.

10. B.O.R. will close at BONN at 09.00 hours and Open at OBERCASSEL at the same hour.

Acknowledge.

(Sd.) W.W

Lieut. A/Adjt.,
51st. Bn. "The King's (Liverpool) Regt.

DISTRIBUTION.

1. Commanding Officer.   7. Lieut. Horrocks.   13. 52nd. K.L.R.
2. 2nd. in Command.   8. Q.M.   14. 12th. L.N.L.
3. Adjutant.   9. T.O.   15. File.
4. O.C. A. Coy.   10. M.O.   16.)
5. O.C. B. Coy.   11. R.S.M.   17.) War Diary.
6. O.C. D. Coy.   12. 1st. King's Bde.

WAR DIARY or INTELLIGENCE SUMMARY.

Army Form C. 2118.

Place	Date	Hour	Summary of Events and Information	Remarks and references to Appendices
BONN	1.10.19		3 ORs to Brigade HQ.	10WB
	2.10.19		Lt H.B. Spencer returned from No 2. Coy A.S.C. 2/Lt J.S. Anderson " " " " "	10WB
	3.10.19			
	4.10.19		2 OR's British Empire Leave Club. - 6 OR's 1st Kings Bde School.	10WB
	5.10.19			

WAR DIARY or INTELLIGENCE SUMMARY.

Army Form C. 2118.

(Erase heading not required.)

Place	Date	Hour	Summary of Events and Information	Remarks and references to Appendices
	6.10.19			
	7.10.19			
	8.10.19			
	9.10.19		2 OR's British Empire Leave Club —	WO's
	10.10.19			

WAR DIARY
or
INTELLIGENCE SUMMARY.
(Erase heading not required.)

Army Form C. 2118.

Place	Date	Hour	Summary of Events and Information	Remarks and references to Appendices
Bonn	11.10.19		1 OR to UK for Demob 4 " transferred to R.A.O.C.	AWB.
	12.10.19		Lt J Roberts returned from Leave 5 ORs to UK for Demob	AWB.
	13.10.19		5 ORs to UK for Demob	AWB.
	14.10.19		Lieut J.H.L. Owen to UK for Demob 4 ORs to UK for Leave. 5 ORs to UK for Demob, 2 ORs to British Empire Leave Club.	AWB

WAR DIARY
or
INTELLIGENCE SUMMARY.
(Erase heading not required.)

Army Form C. 2118.

Instructions regarding War Diaries and Intelligence Summaries are contained in F. S. Regs., Part II. and the Staff Manual respectively. Title pages will be prepared in manuscript.

Place	Date	Hour	Summary of Events and Information	Remarks and references to Appendices
Bonn	15.10.19		4 ORs to U.K. for Leave	W.W.B.
	16.10.19		Capt. & H.S. Roberts to UK for Demob. 4 ORs to U.K. for Leave. 5 ORs to UK for Demob.	W.W.B.
Obercassel	17.10.19		2/Lieut W.Kelly returned from 1st King's Bn Class of Instruction. 1 OR to UK for Demob, 4 ORs to U.K. for Leave. Lieut C.R. Billington returned from Leave.	Battalion move to OBERCASSEL Area. W.W.B. "A"
	18.10.19		4 ORs to U.K. for Leave. 2 ORs to B.E.L.C.	W.W.B.

WAR DIARY or INTELLIGENCE SUMMARY.

Army Form C. 2118.

Place	Date	Hour	Summary of Events and Information	Remarks and references to Appendices
Obercassel	19.10.19		Lieut. J.H.M. Little M.C. to UK for Demob. 2 ORs to British Empire Leave Club.	WWB
			2/Lieut J.B. Anderson. Leave to UK.	
	20.10.19		6 ORs to U.K. for Leave.	WWB.
			1 OR Evac UK Sick	
	21.10.19		Lieut H.B Spencer. Leave to UK	WWB
			2 ORs. to UK for Demob 6 ORs to U.K. for Leave.	
	22.10.19		5 ORs to UK for Demob 6 ORs to U.K. for Leave. WWB.	WWB.
			163 . transferred from 13th K.L.R. Officer transferred from 13th K.L.R.	

WAR DIARY or INTELLIGENCE SUMMARY.

Army Form C. 2118.

Place	Date	Hour	Summary of Events and Information	Remarks and references to Appendices
Obercassel	23.10.19		2/Lt. E Baldwin M.C. DCM. taken on Strength from 13th K.L.R. whilst on Leave.	10WB
			2/Lt L.H. Nicholson Posted to 52nd K.L.R.	
			" H.J Bowyer — — —	
			Lieut. A.H.G. Griggs M.C. to UK for Demob.	
			70 ORs transferred from 13th K.L.R. & taken on Strength accordingly	
			229 " " " to 52nd K.L.R. & struck off Strength "	
			9 " " " from 1st Kings L.T.M.B.	
	24.10.19		Lt. J.E. Stones returned from Ordination Course	10WB
	25.10.19		Lieut. K.D.B. Pocklington to Equipment Guard, Bonn	10WB.
			" S. Lee M.C. — — —	
	26.10.19		2/Lieut J.S. Anderson returned from Leave	10WB.
			2 ORs transferred from 52nd K.L.R.	

WAR DIARY or INTELLIGENCE SUMMARY.

Army Form C. 2118.

(Erase heading not required.)

Place	Date	Hour	Summary of Events and Information	Remarks and references to Appendices
Obercassel	27.10.19			
	28.10.19			
	29.10.19		Lieut. S. Lee M.C. returned from Equipment Guard Bonn. " R.J. Venn proceeded to " " " 1 OR to UK for Leave	WWD3.
	30.10.19		Lieut. A.R. Hayford returned from G.H.Q. Infantry School Strensall Camp UK. 5 OR to UK for Demob.	WWD3
	31.10.19		1 OR transferred to 52nd K.L.R. 2 " to UK for Demob. Leave. Warning order received re Disbandment of Battalion.	WWD3.

www.ingramcontent.com/pod-product-compliance
Lightning Source LLC
Chambersburg PA
CBHW081238170426
43191CB00034B/1971